KENDALL JENNER

A Model's Footprints on the Global Fashion Landscape

Ella Biographix

Table of Content
Introduction

Introduction

The name Kendall Jenner has resonance not only in the world of fashion but also in the dynamic world of celebrity culture, where it represents modernity and progress. Kendall Jenner, who was born on November 3, 1995, into the well-known Kardashian-Jenner family, rose from the shadows of reality television to forge her unique path in the cutthroat worlds of modeling and business.

A compelling story of skill, passion, and unwavering pursuit of her aspirations, Kendall's journey takes place in glamorous fashion magazines and on the charming streets of Los Angeles. She grew up in the spotlight as the second youngest of her siblings and handled the pressures of celebrity with an elegance that belied her age. Kendall's narrative demonstrates her capacity to surpass the stereotypes linked to reality television celebrities and establish herself as a formidable presence in the international fashion sector.

The story of Kendall Jenner's ascent to fame is an intriguing one, characterized by a smooth transition from the glamorous reality TV realm to the sophisticated runways of Paris, Milan, and New York. Her modeling career took off at a young age because she accepted the difficulties of a field that frequently requires both mental and physical toughness. With the help of her mother Kris Jenner, a prosperous entrepreneur in her own right, Kendall set out on a path that would reshape the boundaries of her family's notoriety.

As a style icon, Kendall's attraction comes from both her versatility as a model and her stunning attractiveness. She embraces high fashion seamlessly, appearing on the covers of esteemed fashion magazines and walking the runways for well-known designers. With her distinctive runway walk and sharp features, Kendall has established herself as a symbol of elegance and caught the attention of both photographers and designers.

Beneath the glitzy exterior, Kendall's story is one of resolve and self-control. She had to establish herself beyond her well-known last name because the fashion industry is known for its high standards. Industry insiders like Kendall because she rose to the challenge and developed a strong work ethic and commitment to excellence. Her ability to move between several fashion genres with ease—from streetwear to high couture—testifies to her adaptability and durability in a field notorious for its whimsy. Kendall has an impact that goes beyond the catwalk and into the digital sphere of social media. She has a devoted following on Instagram and Twitter, where fans eagerly await peeks into her opulent life in the era of social media. Expert in the field of self-advertisement, Kendall has used social media to improve her brand and build closer relationships with her followers. Her thoughtfully chosen posts and behind-the-scenes photos provide a carefully chosen insight into the life of a contemporary-style icon.

However, Kendall's story transcends beyond the glamor and sparkle of the fashion industry. She has made the most of her position to advocate for causes that are important to her, lending her voice to concerns about anything from environmental sustainability to mental health awareness. Kendall has shown that she is willing to utilize her position for good in a culture that frequently examines the behavior of individuals in the public eye.

As we read more into Kendall Jenner's life, we find that she was resilient in the face of adversity in addition to being a famous and successful person. The fashion industry's fast-paced environment, the weight of expectations, and public scrutiny have all combined to mold Kendall into the strong woman she is today. There have been many victories and setbacks along the way, and it is only by looking through the prism of these experiences that we can comprehend the lady behind the well-known name on a deeper level.

The chapters that follow take us on a journey through the life of Kendall Jenner, examining the crucial choices, life-changing events, and complex web of relationships that have molded her into the complex individual she is today. Kendall's story is a compelling narrative that goes beyond the surface, allowing readers to see the development of a young woman who has handled the complications of celebrity with grace and candor. From the shimmering lights of the runway to the quiet moments of self-discovery.

Chapter 1: Early Life

Raised in the well-known Kardashian-Jenner family around the world, Kendall experienced a combination of luxury, the spotlight, and the difficulties of being a public figure in her early years.

It was clear from the minute Kendall Jenner was born that her life would be different from everyone else's. Having been born into the large Kardashian-Jenner family, whose sisters are already well-known in the entertainment world, Kendall's birth was truly remarkable. Los Angeles, a city where dreams are both formed and broken, provided the colorful and lavish background for her early years.

Family Background

Being the second youngest member of the Kardashian-Jenner family, she comes from a family known for reality TV, fashion, and business. Her family's complex background has greatly shaped who she is and how her profession has developed.

Kendall Jenner had a unique upbringing as the daughter of Kris Jenner and Caitlyn Jenner, who was once known as Bruce Jenner. She experienced growing up in the spotlight thanks to the hugely successful reality TV program "Keeping Up with the Kardashians," where she had to deal with the pressures of puberty and continuous media attention. Critics and fans both praised and criticized her family's dynamics for their honest depiction of her personal life.

The matriarch Kris Jenner skillfully managed their public image, which helped the Kardashian-Jenner family rise to notoriety. Through Kris, Kendall's mother's side can claim Armenian ancestry, which gives her background even more cultural depth. Astute entrepreneur Kris built the Kardashian-Jenner company, transforming the family's lifestyle into a brand that transcended the TV screen.

Caitlyn Jenner, the Olympic gold medallist in decathlon, added an athletic element to Kendall's family history through her influence. Later in life, Caitlyn underwent a gender change that was a major turning point in the family's narrative and contributed to discussions on gender identity and acceptance worldwide. This life-changing event demonstrated the family's adaptability and mutual support during significant life transitions.

Kendall's siblings—younger sister Kylie Jenner and half-sisters Kim, Kourtney, and Khloé Kardashian—all helped to shape the complex family dynamic. The sisters' strong relationship, which was frequently seen in their joint endeavors and public appearances, supported the notion of a close-knit family. Global audiences were able to relate to the complicated real-life dynamics reflected in the on-screen family relationships, complete with arguments and reconciliations.

In Kendall's life, the family's ties to the fashion and cosmetics industries became more evident. Her remarkable beauty and tall size allowed her to enter the modeling industry at a young age. As she appeared on the covers of prominent magazines and walked the runways for well-known designers, Kendall solidified her reputation as a major player in the fashion industry. Kendall's ascent to the top of the fashion industry was surely impacted by the Kardashian-Jenner brand, which is known for its glitz and flair.

One major influence on Kendall's understanding of personal identity was her father, Caitlyn Jenner. Conversations concerning gender expression and acceptance gained momentum as a result of Caitlyn's open path of self-discovery and authenticity. Consequently, Kendall became a champion for inclusivity in the fashion business, leveraging her influence to encourage diversity and question conventional notions of beauty.

Even with the Kardashian-Jenner family's glamor and splendor, Kendall has had her share of difficulties. Resilience and a strong sense of self have been necessary to manage a public profession under continual criticism. Undoubtedly, navigating the challenges of celebrity within the framework of her family's legacy has molded Kendall's personality and highlighted the value of authenticity in a society where perceptions are often the driving force.

Childhood and Education

Kendall had a strong interest in fashion and modeling from a young age. She first came to public attention as a young girl, appearing on the reality TV series "Keeping Up with the Kardashians." The program, which chronicled the Kardashian-Jenner family's everyday activities, gave Kendall an early introduction to the workings of the entertainment industry.

Engulfed in a culture that emphasized beauty and style, Kendall grew up in the fast-paced metropolis of Los Angeles. She became interested in the world of fashion maybe because of this setting. She used to go to a lot of events, red-carpet appearances, and fashion shows with her elder sisters, which gave her an early introduction to the field that would become her career.

Kendall's family stressed the value of education despite the attraction of the entertainment sector. She went to the esteemed private school Sierra Canyon School in the Los Angeles region, just like her siblings. There were difficulties in juggling a burgeoning public career with academic obligations, but Kendall handled this precarious balance with grace.

Kendall's modeling career took off as she moved through her adolescent years. Wilhelmina Models and The Society Management were among the prominent modeling agencies with whom she signed. With these calculated actions, Kendall made a significant shift from being a reality TV star to a major participant in the fashion industry. In a field that prizes individuality, her striking appearance and tall stature made her stand out, and she soon became in high demand as a model for high-profile advertising campaigns.

In addition to her family's early fashion exposure and her TV appearances, Kendall pursued modeling with a strong sense of purpose and commitment. In the cutthroat world of high fashion, she made a name for herself as a top model by walking the catwalks for prominent labels like Chanel, Givenchy, and Marc Jacobs.

Even as her modeling career took off, Kendall never wavered in her dedication to her studies in addition to her professional obligations. In 2014, she earned her diploma from Sierra Canyon School, demonstrating her ability to balance the demands of both academia and celebrity. Kendall's choice to put her studies first in addition to her growing modeling career demonstrated an admirable commitment to intellectual and personal development.

Over the next few years, Kendall Jenner's career took off. She rose to prominence as a worldwide fashion star, working with well-known designers and appearing on the covers of major fashion magazines. Her accomplishments in commercial endeavors such as her partnerships with several fashion and beauty firms demonstrated her versatility in addition to her success in modeling.

Kendall's early years and schooling were crucial in forming her success and identity. Her upbringing in the Kardashian-Jenner household, education at an esteemed university, and pursuit of a modeling career all came together to pave the way for her success in the entertainment and fashion industries. Kendall Jenner became a role model for aspirants by skillfully fusing her love of fashion with her dedication to school, showing that success in the public spotlight can coexist with a commitment to personal growth and academic endeavors.

Chapter 2: Modeling Career

A thoughtful and calculated approach to her work has contributed to Kendall's climb to fame as a model. She emerged from the shadows of her reality TV past and made a name for herself in the fashion industry. In addition to her obvious beauty, Kendall's charm comes from her ability to approach the business with sincere enthusiasm and dedication.

The main thing that makes Kendall unique as a model is how adaptable she is. She moves fluidly between several areas of the fashion spectrum, from high couture runways to advertising campaigns.

Entry into Modeling

Acquiring a career in modeling typically requires a trifecta of skill, luck, and determination. One well-known person who has accomplished this is Kendall Jenner, who is a part of the well-known Kardashian-Jenner family. The interesting story of Kendall's ascent to stardom in the modeling profession illuminates the workings of the fashion industry and the difficulties experienced by aspiring models. The fact that Kendall Jenner comes from a well-known family did not propel her into the modeling industry. Being a member of the Kardashian-Jenner family certainly helped, but Kendall still needed to establish herself as a legitimate competitor in the fiercely cutthroat fashion industry. Her ability to make the most of her current platform and carve out a niche for herself in the market is a crucial component of her success.

When Kendall signed with the prestigious modeling agency The Society Management in 2013, her modeling career took a significant change. By taking this calculated risk, she demonstrated that modeling was more than just a passing interest. Kendall's affiliation with The Society Management gave her access to highly sought-after possibilities in the fashion industry. Agencies have a significant influence on the course of a model's career.

An important turning point that demonstrated Kendall's ability as a high-end model was her runway debut. She was able to establish credibility in the industry by walking for well-known designers during the fashion weeks in New York, Paris, and Milan. Designers, casting directors, and fashion fans were all immediately drawn to her statuesque form, beautiful features, and confident runway presence.

Apart from her achievements in the runway industry, Kendall also left her mark in editorial and commercial modeling. She proved to be a versatile model by participating in high-profile ads for international brands, representing a range of styles and sensibilities. Her work with well-known stylists and photographers strengthened her reputation in the fashion industry and made her a sought-after model for commercial and editorial projects.

The significance of social media in Kendall Jenner's modeling career is one important factor. Nowadays, social media presence and influence are just as important to models as physical characteristics and runway skills when evaluating them in the digital age.

With a sizable fan base on social media sites like Instagram, Kendall made good use of it to interact with fans, give behind-the-scenes looks at her modeling business, and promote products. In addition to boosting her notoriety, this internet persona demonstrated how the fashion industry was changing.

Even though Kendall Jenner had a lot of success when she first started modeling, it's important to recognize the difficulties she had. For its lack of openness and diversity, the fashion industry has historically come under fire. Kendall's success and the success of other models from other origins have gradually changed industry norms, encouraging more representation.

One distinguishing characteristic of Kendall Jenner in handling the challenging modeling industry is her dedication to professionalism and flexibility. Apart from her physical attractiveness, her ability to work with different creative teams, accept the ever-changing nature of fashion, and adjust to varied trends have all contributed significantly to her continued relevance in the business.

Major Runway Shows

Big runway shows are essential occasions in the fashion industry because they provide designers with a stage on which to present their most recent collections to an international audience. Of all the runway models, Kendall Jenner's name is one that always sticks out. Her appearance on the catwalk is evidence of her extraordinary work ethic and adaptability in the fashion industry, in addition to her genetic gifts.

As a member of the well-known Kardashian-Jenner family, Kendall Jenner has grown to be a powerful figure in the modeling industry. Numerous high-profile participation in significant fashion events across the world have preceded her runway career. Jenner has made a lasting impression on the fashion business by walking the catwalks of some of the most prestigious houses, from New York to Paris.

The versatility of Kendall Jenner's runway career is seen in her ability to fit into a wide range of styles and aesthetics with ease. Jenner consistently exhibits a wonderful chameleon-like skill, whether she's walking the catwalk in avant-garde designs or looking elegant in high couture. Because of her versatility, she has been a sought-after model for many different designers, solidifying her reputation as a style icon.

One of the most important occasions on the fashion calendar, New York Fashion Week, has been a regular platform for Kendall Jenner. The dynamic environment and cutting-edge designers of the city offer the perfect stage for her to display her runway skills. Jenner has walked for a variety of designers during this legendary week, from well-known brands to up-and-coming artists, adding to the diverse tapestry of styles that characterizes the occasion.

Jenner relocated to Paris, the global center of fashion, and made a lasting impression on the catwalks of renowned labels. The sophisticated and innovative reputation of the City of Light fits in perfectly with Kendall Jenner's personal style preferences.

She adds a sense of contemporary elegance to the classic charm of the Paris fashion scene as she walks the runway for well-known French design labels.

Jenner participates in significant runway events outside of the traditional fashion calendar. She has consistently appeared in much-awaited occasions such as the Victoria's Secret Fashion Show, where she not only graces the runway but also personifies the pinnacle of elegance and seduction. The spectacular lingerie displays and intricate themes of the Victoria's Secret runway offer Jenner a distinctive stage on which to highlight her flexibility as a model. Apart from her distinct runway shows, Kendall Jenner has served as an inspiration for fashion designers who aim to innovate and expand the limits of the industry.

Working with renowned designers has allowed her to contribute as a muse as well as a model, inspiring and influencing the direction of collections. Jenner's standing in the fashion industry has increased as a result of the mutually beneficial relationship between the model and designer, which has made her a sought-after presence on the catwalk.

Major runway shows have an impact that extends beyond the immediate spectacle; they influence and mirror the changing face of fashion. Jenner's involvement in these presentations is a cultural statement more than just an outfit show. Her social media following is enormous, and her runway shows can change perceptions of beauty and impact fashion trends.

The trajectory of Kendall Jenner's runway career also highlights how diversity and representation in the fashion industry are changing. Her appearance on well-known runways helps to shatter stereotypes by demonstrating that beauty is universal and transcends social boundaries. Given that Jenner is a model and has navigated a profession that is frequently criticized for its lack of inclusivity, her career sets the standard for increased diversity and acceptance in the fashion industry.

Big runway shows aim to create moments that are memorable and meaningful for the audience, not only for the garments. With her natural grace and commanding presence, Kendall Jenner has played a key role in creating these kinds of runway moments. Jenner can add a unique vitality to any style, drawing attention from spectators, whether it's a stunning couture gown or a cutting-edge streetwear combo.

Chapter 3: Fashion Influencer

The role of influencers in the ever-changing world of fashion has grown in importance, as they shape trends and prescribe styles. Among the notable people in this scene, Kendall Jenner is a shining example of contemporary fashion influence; she rose from her reality television beginnings to become a major player in the business.

Style Evolution

Being a prominent model and a part of the well-known Kardashian-Jenner family, Jenner's fashion path has captured the interest of both admirers and detractors. From her early roles on "Keeping Up with the Kardashians" to her well-known runway walks, Kendall's style development is a reflection of both her development and the fast-paced dynamics of the fashion industry. The glossy image that her family projected on their reality TV program during Kendall's early years of public exposure greatly affected her style. The young celebrity was known for wearing trendy clothing, statement accessories, and patterns that were popular at the time and were associated with the Kardashian-Jenner look. She skillfully balanced her youthful energy and the refined demeanor required of a member of one of the most well-known families in show business during her adolescent years.

However, Kendall started to establish her sense of style in the modeling industry. Her appearance changed drastically when she moved from reality TV to high-end runway shows. Jenner began experimenting with her clothing, adding avant-garde designs, neutral hues, and sleek silhouettes as she embraced the sophisticated and minimalistic aesthetics of the fashion elite. Her runway shows for high-end labels like Givenchy and Chanel presented a model who was not only stunning but also had an acute sense of high fashion.

The ability of Kendall Jenner to transition between different fashion identities with ease is one of the main components of her style progression. Whether Kendall is strutting the red carpet in a stunning gown or slaying the streets in easygoing yet stylish ensembles, her adaptability never fails to please a wide range of viewers. Her ability to adapt has come to define her fashion path, enabling her to move with ease through many fashion environments.

Kendall's style changed along with the fashion industry. She welcomed the emergence of streetwear and athleisure, combining elements of utility and comfort into her wardrobe selections. Her off-duty style became characterized by sporty costumes mixed with opulent accessories, exhibiting a modern and approachable aspect of her style that appealed to a younger audience.

Beyond what she wears, Kendall Jenner's style has evolved greatly due to her attractiveness and personal grooming habits. Her change in hairstyles from long, flowing locks to shorter, more edgy looks reflected her exploration of many fashion statements. Jenner's hairstyle decisions became essential to her overall style story, regardless of whether she chose a sleek bob or embraced the carefree beauty of disheveled waves.

Notably, Kendall's style growth reflects not just specific fashion moments but also broader cultural trends and evolving industry norms. As diversity and inclusivity gained traction in the fashion industry, Kendall and her contemporaries joined a movement that embraced a wider variety of beauty standards. This change impacted not just the models chosen for fashion shows but also Jenner's personal style expression, as she adopted a more representative and inclusive stance.

Kendall Jenner has persisted in pushing the limits of style in recent years, adopting daring and nontraditional outfits that defy accepted conventions. Her partnerships with well-known brands and designers have cemented her position as a style icon, and many aspiring fashionistas find inspiration in her evolving sense of style.

Collaborations and Endorsements

Jenner, who is well-known for her modeling profession, moved from reality television to become a style icon around the world with ease. In the cutthroat worlds of entertainment and fashion, her shrewd alliances and sponsorships have been crucial in securing her place.

In the context of Kendall Jenner's profession, collaborations go beyond simple brand affiliations. They embody a mutually beneficial relationship between her brand and the values of the businesses she supports. Her long-standing partnership with the prestigious fashion house Calvin Klein is one such partnership. As the brand's face, Jenner has starred in multiple ads and played a significant role in capturing the contemporary, minimalist aesthetic of the company.

Jenner collaborates with projects outside of fashion. She has entered the beauty business, forming alliances that fit with her reputation as a trailblazer. Her partnership with Estée Lauder, where she served as the face of the company's beauty ads, is a great example. Through this collaboration, she was able to demonstrate her versatility and establish herself as a widely recognized beauty influencer.

Conversely, endorsements move into the area of ambassadorship and product marketing. Jenner frequently supports her endeavors in addition to the conventional ones. Her support for the tequila brand 818 contributes to its growth. Jenner has shown the value of celebrity endorsement in influencing consumer perceptions and increasing product visibility by actively taking part in the brand's advertising.

Regarding the fashion industry, Jenner's partnership with Adidas is significant. As the company's global spokesperson, she has played a key role in giving the sportswear behemoth a more modern and youthful look. Her fashion prominence has increased as a result of the partnership, which has also increased Adidas' appeal to younger consumers.

When it comes to partnerships and endorsements, Kendall Jenner stands out for her ability to work with companies that share her beliefs and sense of style.

Customers connect with this honesty, which builds a sense of trust that goes beyond a simple celebrity endorsement. Jenner's selections in partnerships show a conscious attempt to positively impact the industries she participates with, whether it is through her support of inclusive beauty campaigns or her connection with environmentally responsible firms.

Additionally, social media has been essential in enhancing the influence of Kendall Jenner's partnerships and sponsorships. She is a living example of influencer marketing in the modern era, having amassed a sizable following on social media sites like Instagram. Every post turns into a possible marketing tool as she skillfully incorporates the recommended goods into her style and way of life. Through this digital presence, she can directly communicate with a worldwide audience, expanding the scope and efficacy of her collaborations.

Jenner frequently signs endorsement contracts that go above and beyond expectations. Her association with firms such as Apple in the technology sector demonstrates her versatility beyond conventional industry classifications. This diversity demonstrates how celebrity endorsements are changing, with influencers like Jenner in great demand not just for their appeal in particular markets but also for their general cross-industry influence.

It's crucial to remember, though, that not every endorsement and partnership has been without controversy. Like many celebrities, Jenner has occasionally been the target of criticism and investigation, especially when her affiliations with certain social and political causes have crossed paths. Handling these obstacles is a necessary component of running a high-profile job, and the way celebrities handle these circumstances greatly affects their public perception.

Chapter 4: Business Ventures

Kendall's entry into the beauty sector is one of her noteworthy endeavors. Kendall started her brand of beauty goods by utilizing her enormous social media following and her global impact. Her brand, which offers everything from skincare routines to beauty basics, embodies her dedication to diversity and quality. In a field that frequently has representational issues, Kendall has succeeded in carving out a niche for herself by embracing diversity in her product offerings.

Kendall + Kylie Collection

Since its launch, the renowned American sisters Kendall and Kylie Jenner have been leading forces behind the Kendall + Kylie Collection, which has caused quite a stir in the fashion world. The pair, well-known for their exquisite taste and powerful presence in pop culture, has effectively converted their vision into a fashion line that appeals to a wide range of consumers.

The aim behind Kendall and Kylie Jenner's partnership, with two well-known models and TV personalities, was to create a collection that would reflect their respective tastes while also having a unified and adaptable appeal. The Kendall + Kylie Collection, which debuted in 2015, immediately became well-known for its modern styles, avant-garde silhouettes, and mix of dressy and casual pieces that suit a variety of fashion tastes.

The Kendall + Kylie Collection's ability to expertly combine refinement with an effortlessly cool appearance is one of its distinguishing features. By incorporating aspects of streetwear inspiration and tailored elegance into their creations, the sisters have successfully captured the spirit of modern femininity. The collection has been increasingly popular among fashionistas of all ages due to this distinctive blend.

The collection has an eclectic mix of dresses, shirts, bottoms, outerwear, and accessories, demonstrating the adaptability that has come to be associated with the Jenner sisters' style. The Kendall + Kylie Collection appeals to a wide range of fashion sensibilities with everything from elegant, everyday clothing that radiates a comfortable yet sophisticated mood to sleek, minimalist pieces perfect for red-carpet events.

Especially, the Kendall + Kylie Collection, which features fitness items that sexily combine comfort and flair, has left its imprint on the athleisure scene. The sisters' grasp of the changing fashion scene and the increasing desire for adaptable, practical clothes that can be worn for both casual outings and the gym is evident in the inclusion of trendy athleisure outfits.

Partnerships with well-known stores and online fashion communities have increased the Kendall + Kylie Collection's influence and audience. Through the strategic use of their massive social media following and influence, Kendall and Kylie Jenner have built a brand that appeals to people all over the world. The collection has become extremely successful since it is easily accessible to fans and fashion aficionados across the globe through its multiple online platforms.

Apart from its triumph in the apparel sector, the Kendall + Kylie Collection has broadened its scope to encompass an assortment of accessories that harmonize with the brand's overall style. The sisters' dedication to quality and style is evident in the meticulous craftsmanship of their purses, shoes, and eyewear. The accessories improve the collection's overall coherence in addition to acting as statement pieces.

With a wide selection of shoes that capture the sisters' unique style, the Kendall + Kylie brand has also entered the footwear market. The footwear line of the Jenner sisters reflects their ability to accommodate a wide range of fashion tastes, from beautiful heels that radiate elegance to cozy and fashionable sneakers.

The sisters' impact on fashion trends has come to be associated with the Kendall + Kylie Collection, even outside of the actual merchandise. As trendsetters in the industry, Kendall and Kylie Jenner have made a name for themselves with their sharp sense of developing fashions and dedication to being ahead of the curve. The collection's designs frequently include the newest runway trends while still feeling timeless, guaranteeing its continued relevance in the rapidly evolving fashion industry.

Entrepreneurial Pursuits

Kendall Jenner's success in the fashion sector is the cornerstone of her entrepreneurial path. Making use of her modeling profession, she has appeared on the covers of big fashion magazines, walked the catwalks for esteemed brands, and collaborated with them. In addition to posing for numerous fashion ads, Kendall has dabbled in fashion design. She has proven her ability to manage the challenging and competitive fashion industry through her engagement in developing profitable fashion lines and her partnerships with renowned designers.

One of Kendall Jenner's most well-known business ventures is the fashion label she co-founded, Kendall + Kylie, with her younger sister Kylie. This project demonstrates Kendall's astute perception of current fashion trends and her capacity to engage a wide range of people. The collection features a variety of apparel, accessories, and shoes that are a reflection of Kendall's sense of style and sense of fashion. She has established herself as a major player in the fashion industry and helped shape trends and the tastes of a global audience with this endeavor.

Kendall has shown a keen interest in the skincare and cosmetics sectors in addition to her fashion endeavors. Her association with skincare goods, such as her position as a Proactiv brand ambassador, demonstrates her capacity to match her brand with causes and products. Kendall's collaborations and endorsement arrangements in the beauty industry demonstrate her ability to take advantage of economic possibilities and leverage her influence in the fashion and beauty industries.

Beyond the fields of beauty and fashion, entrepreneurship is another area of interest for Kendall Jenner. She has carefully cultivated relationships with a variety of brands, from beverage and technology companies to lifestyle and wellness items, by leveraging her social media presence. Her diversification of collaborations highlights her capacity to adapt and her commercial acumen as she understands the value of using her influence to benefit various businesses.

Moreover, Kendall's interest in the beverage industry is evident from her involvement in the tequila business. She has delved into the spirits industry, demonstrating her openness to explore new and diversified industries, having co-founded 818 Tequila. Kendall's entrepreneurial zeal is evident in the introduction of 818 Tequila, as she is actively involved in all aspects of the brand's operations, from marketing to production. This endeavor displays her as a businesswoman with a talent for seeing new opportunities and gives her portfolio of entrepreneurial endeavors another depth.

Beyond her endeavors, Kendall Jenner has embraced the teamwork-oriented nature of entrepreneurship. Her participation in partnerships and joint ventures with other business owners demonstrates her capacity for teamwork in professional environments. These partnerships help her firm grow while also fostering the development of cutting-edge experiences and goods that appeal to a broad market.

Kendall's ability to go beyond the confines of her initial success and notoriety in the entertainment sector is a defining characteristic of her entrepreneurial journey. Her business endeavors demonstrate a calculated approach to brand building, leveraging her influence and personal brand to expand her line of business. Beyond appearances, Kendall Jenner's entrepreneurship success stems from her ability to recognize possibilities, make calculated choices, and carve out a significant niche for herself in a variety of industries.

Chapter 5: Personal Life

In addition to her remarkable beauty and prosperous career, Kendall Jenner, the well-known American model and television personality, has captured the attention of millions of people with her intimate views of her personal life.

Relationships

While Kendall Jenner, the oldest daughter of Kris and Caitlyn Jenner, has succeeded in making her name for herself in the modeling world, many have taken an interest in her private life. In this analysis of Kendall Jenner's romantic partnerships, we look at the dynamics, difficulties, and public perception of her relationships.

With numerous high-profile partnerships making headlines, Kendall Jenner's dating history is a veritable open book. One of her earliest well-known partnerships was with British singer Harry Styles, who is a part of the worldwide phenomenon One Direction. Although they never formally acknowledged their relationship, the couple's public appearances and intimate moments stoked suspicions that they were dating back in 2013. The strong media coverage of their relationship brought to light the difficulties of leading a private life while in the public eye.

Kendall developed relationships with several other well-known people as her modeling career took off. As their friendship with NBA player Ben Simmons grew, people frequently saw the two out at events together. But it's well known that the demands of popularity and hectic schedules can make it harder to keep up a relationship, particularly when one or both of the partners are well-known.

Celebrities rarely have privacy, and Kendall Jenner is no exception. Any relationship may become more strained as a result of the public's and media's constant monitoring. In this sense, social media sites are both helpful and detrimental. They give celebrities a way to interact with their admirers, but they also give the general public a forum on which to analyze and conjecture about their private lives. It can be difficult to build and maintain a sincere connection because Kendall's relationships are frequently the subject of gossip articles and social media debates.

It's important to remember that, despite the intense scrutiny from the media and the public, celebrities—like Kendall Jenner—are just regular people trying to figure out what it means to love and be in relationships. Sometimes the public's interest in celebrities' personal lives eclipses their accomplishments in the workplace and the subtleties of their personalities. The representation of them in the media may not always accurately represent their experiences.

Similar to numerous individuals in her cohort, Kendall Jenner belongs to a contemporary epoch whereby romantic connections transpire not just behind closed doors but also via social media. Her followers are privy to carefully chosen moments in her life, which add to the story of her relationships. The narrative incorporates her Instagram pictures, tweets, and Snapchat stories, allowing both admirers and detractors to comment on the highs and lows of her amorous journey.

In the world Kendall lives in, there can be particularly strong pressure to live up to conventional standards of success and attractiveness. Public views of her compatibility, attractiveness, and success in relationships get entwined with the story, adding to the pressure she faces. High-profile couples can face restrictive expectations, which makes it difficult for them to truly express their individuality while living under constant public scrutiny.

Kendall Jenner's love experience serves as an example of the special set of abilities needed to navigate relationships in the public glare. When both partners are in the spotlight, maintaining the delicate balance between their private and public lives becomes even more difficult. The difficulty lies not just in controlling the interactions between two people but also in resolving the outside variables that affect their partnership.

Despite the difficulties, Kendall Jenner has demonstrated fortitude in retaining her identity in the face of celebrity. Even while her relationships are in public view, they also demonstrate her capacity to handle the difficulties of love in the spotlight. She has had to grow and learn from her experiences, just like any other person, and each relationship has probably had an impact on how she views love and companionship.

Public Persona

Born into the Kardashian-Jenner family, she has become a prosperous model, businesswoman, and influencer, savvily negotiating the treacherous terrain of celebrity with a measured approach.

The foundation of Kendall's public identity is her modeling profession, which began to take off when she was a teenager. She abandoned her family's history in reality TV and entered the fashion industry with a tenacity that has come to define her approach to her work. Her distinctive runway presence, which combines refinement and effortless elegance, draws the attention of well-known designers and secures her a place at the top of the industry.

Outside of the runway, Kendall's public profile has been heavily reliant on her ability to build a unique image. She frequently exudes a sense of subtle elegance, choosing a minimalist style that appeals to her enormous fan base as well as the fashion industry, in contrast to her more flamboyant brothers. This calculated stylistic decision is both a personal statement and a calculated attempt to stand out from the family, which is well-known for its extravagant and publicized way of living.

The combination of Kendall's public persona with her business endeavors enhances the public perception of her. Using her enormous social media following, she has successfully started several businesses, ranging from joint partnerships with well-known brands to her projects. This business sense has enhanced Kendall's professional portfolio and strengthened the belief that she is a smart, independent person who can successfully navigate the cutthroat entertainment industry.

Kendall Jenner has perfected the art of building a digital identity that connects with millions of people in the era of social media domination. With millions of followers, her Instagram feed offers a meticulously managed look into her life through a mix of personal moments, behind-the-scenes photos, and high-fashion editorials that bring a human touch to the glossy image. Through the deliberate use of social media, she maintains the aspirational appeal that characterizes her public persona while simultaneously cultivating a feeling of intimacy with her supporters.

With her entry into activism, Kendall has expanded her public profile and shown that she cares about social issues in addition to the flash and glamor of the fashion industry. She has used her platform to address important issues, whether she is fighting for social justice or environmental reasons, balancing her public persona with a feeling of duty and knowledge. Her involvement in social issues highlights her diverse identity outside of the modeling industry and appeals to a socially concerned audience.

Even with her well-constructed public persona, Kendall Jenner has encountered criticism and controversy. The focus on her private life, romantic affairs, and purported scandals has never left her. She does, however, add to the narrative of maturity and resilience through her capacity to handle these storms with a cool head and selective disclosure, which further shapes the public's opinion of her.

Within the world of brand collaborations and endorsements, Kendall's public persona has shown to be a valuable resource. Her reputation as a sought-after ambassador and her affiliation with well-known brands increase the image's commercial value. In addition to supporting her financial success, this synergy between her brand and corporate endorsements serves to further solidify Kendall's reputation as a trailblazer and tastemaker.

Chapter 6: Controversies

During Kendall Jenner's career, a notable scandal included the 2017 Pepsi commercial debacle. The commercial, which sought to promote harmony and understanding, was met with strong criticism since it was seen as trivializing social justice movements, especially the Black Lives Matter movement. Kendall Jenner, who had a major part in the advertisement, drew criticism for it; many said that she was exploiting important social concerns for profit. In addition to harming Kendall's reputation, the uproar caused Pepsi to remove the advertisement and apologize.

Media Scrutiny

Media scrutiny nowadays is heavily reliant on media scrutiny, and people like Kendall

Jenner frequently find themselves the target of unrelenting public scrutiny. Kendall Jenner, who comes from the well-known Kardashian-Jenner family throughout the world, has made a name for herself in the entertainment business and has drawn equal parts praise and criticism.

The complicated relationship between celebrities and the public is at the center of media attention. Information on celebrities is always available thanks to social media sites, tabloids, and entertainment news sources, and Kendall Jenner is no different. A fascinated public has followed Jenner's every step, from her early days as a reality TV star on "Keeping Up with the Kardashians" to her development as a prosperous model and influencer.

Kendall Jenner's modeling career has been the subject of public attention. She made her debut in the very competitive world of fashion and rapidly became well-known, appearing on the covers of esteemed fashion magazines and walking the runways of famous designers. But this achievement also brought increased scrutiny. Both detractors and admirers keep a tight eye on her wardrobe choices, analyzing each item of clothing she chooses, analyzing her runway shows, and conjecturing her influence on contemporary fashion trends.

It is impossible to overestimate the influence of social media on the level of media scrutiny. With millions of followers on social media sites like Instagram and Twitter, Kendall Jenner's posts and behaviors frequently elicit strong, instantaneous responses. Positive and bad comments pour into her social media accounts, intensifying the scrutiny due to this rapid feedback loop. Celebrities live in a time where they are not only stars but also influencers; as such, the media scrutinizes them constantly and their every move has the power to mold public opinion.

The investigation dives into Jenner's private life in addition to the glitzy exterior of the fashion industry. Because of the close-up view into the Kardashian-Jenner family's life that the reality program offered, the world has seen intimate details of Kendall Jenner's connections, relationships, and personal issues. Because of her transparency, the public and media have been free to criticize and pass judgment on her decisions and deeds.

Furthermore, the media pays more attention to Kendall Jenner's troubles because of their intersection. Every action she makes, whether it's tackling societal issues, public feuds, or corporate alliances, becomes a talking point. Media sources frequently analyze her words and deeds, and the public dialog surrounding her becomes a mirror of larger societal discussions.

The intense focus on Kendall Jenner highlights broader problems in the entertainment sector, like the pressure on stars to uphold a particular image. Constant exposure to criticism from the public can be detrimental to mental health, increasing stress and anxiety. Celebrities endure more difficulties because of the need to live up to social norms about success and beauty, which emphasizes the need for a more complex knowledge of the person behind the celebrity image.

Kendall Jenner has periodically resorted to actively addressing controversies to manage media attention. She makes an effort to take command of her story and give her actions some perspective, whether via public remarks, social media posts, or interviews. This tactic is not without its difficulties, though, as attempts at clarification might not always have the desired effect and public opinion can be erratic.

The media's focus on Kendall Jenner is a microcosm of the larger problems facing society and the entertainment industry. It depicts the mutually beneficial interaction that exists between the public and celebrities, in which notoriety attracts both praise and criticism. It is important for people in the limelight as well as the audience who consume and engage with the stories the media creates to comprehend the mechanics of media scrutiny.

Challenges in the Spotlight

Despite being from the well-known Kardashian-Jenner family, she has faced obstacles on her path to success. Being in the spotlight since a young age has presented Jenner with unique and difficult difficulties, from navigating the complexity of celebrity to overcoming personal struggles.

The continual strain and scrutiny that come with belonging to one of the most well-known families in the world has been a major issue for Kendall Jenner. The Kardashian-Jenner family is no stranger to the spotlight, and the public closely monitors every decision they make. For Kendall, this entails addressing persistent rumors about her personal life in addition to the demands that come with being a model and public personality. Her constant attention on social media and the unrelenting paparazzi have made it difficult for her to keep her solitude.

Within the fashion world, Kendall has had her share of challenges. She has had to overcome doubts from people who doubted her ability as a model and believed that her fame was the only reason for her success despite having a great modeling career. Critics disregarded her talent and hard work, claiming that her family's connections gave her an advantage in the field. Kendall felt pressured by this task to continually prove herself and carve out a niche for herself outside of the Kardashian-Jenner brand.

In addition, the fashion industry itself has particular difficulties. Models are under a lot of pressure to live up to specific standards due to the fierce competition and constantly changing beauty standards. With her unique style, Kendall has had to negotiate these expectations without sacrificing her uniqueness. Maintaining a particular image and reputation that is consistent with the brand she represents is just as important as looking good.

Her involvement in several incidents has also brought attention to one aspect of Kendall Jenner's life. Kendall has received criticism several times, whether it be from dubious advertisements, controversial social media posts, or her involvement in particular events. In the era of social media, handling these disputes can be especially difficult because public opinion can change quickly and harshly. For someone who is in the spotlight all the time, mastering the art of handling and responding to these situations with grace is a constant challenge.

Beyond outside influences, Kendall has been transparent about her experiences with anxiety. It can be particularly challenging to identify and treat mental health issues in a society that expects perfection. It can be difficult for people like Kendall to get therapy without worrying about stigma or judgment because of the expectation to maintain a perfect public image, which can worsen these problems. This problem serves as a reminder of the need for mental health awareness in the entertainment sector and the necessity of de-stigmatizing discussions about mental health.

Problems with family dynamics can arise even in the close-knit Kardashian-Jenner family. Kendall, like her siblings, has had to negotiate the challenges of upholding family ties while simultaneously managing individual aspirations. Juggling personal relationships with the demands of celebrity can be a tricky undertaking. The family's notoriety has frequently resulted in close public monitoring of their relationships, which has made their personal lives even more difficult.

Kendall Jenner has also turned into a supporter of environmental and social causes in recent years. Although this is a good thing, it also presents new difficulties. It takes considerable consideration to use one's platform to address global concerns without coming across as performative activism. Kendall has had to make her way through this terrain, making sure that her dedication to environmental and social problems is sincere and knowledgeable.

Chapter 7: Philanthropy

Known for her modeling profession and ties to the Kardashian-Jenner family, Kendall Jenner has regularly utilized her platform to support different humanitarian organizations and bring attention to social issues. Her philanthropic endeavors demonstrate her determination to use her power to advance societal progress.

Social Causes

Being a part of the well-known Kardashian-Jenner family, Kendall has used her platform to advocate for and raise awareness of causes that align with her moral principles and the more general social challenges of the day.

Mental health awareness is one important concern that Kendall Jenner has advocated for. Kendall has been transparent about her battles with anxiety, which may be detrimental to an individual's well-being in a world where the demands of celebrity and continuous public scrutiny can be overwhelming. She has helped de-stigmatize mental health concerns by exposing her personal experiences, inspiring others to get treatment, and cultivating empathy for the struggles many people confront behind the glittering façade of celebrity life.

Additionally, Kendall Jenner has taken a leading role in environmental sustainability activities. Celebrities like Kendall can spread the word about environmental conservation as climate change becomes a more pressing worldwide issue. Through her platform, Kendall has promoted eco-friendly behaviors including wearing sustainable clothing and increasing public awareness of how human activity affects the environment. By doing this, she has inspired her fans to live more ecologically friendly lives and support the continuous efforts to protect the planet's natural resources.

Kendall Jenner has supported racial justice and the Black Lives Matter movement in addition to mental health and environmental sustainability. Kendall used her platform to speak out against racial injustice in reaction to the worldwide rallies against institutional racism and instances of police brutality. She participated in campaigns to advance equality and destroy discriminatory structures, posted educational materials on social media, and promoted conversation on racial issues.

Kendall is a philanthropist who supports a variety of organizations. She has actively supported numerous philanthropic groups and allied herself with causes that tackle a broad spectrum of social challenges. Kendall has shown a dedication to having a beneficial social influence, whether it is by aiding in disaster relief operations, fostering education in impoverished places, or sponsoring children's hospitals.

In addition, Kendall Jenner's advocacy for LGBTQ+ rights is deserving of notice. She has continuously shown her support for the LGBTQ+ community and has made use of her position to promote acceptance and inclusivity. Through her participation in Pride events and her partnerships with LGBTQ+ rights organizations, Kendall has made a positive impact on promoting tolerance and inclusivity in society.

It's important to recognize that controversy has occasionally surrounded Kendall Jenner's advocacy activities. Celebrities who support social issues are frequently the target of criticism, with some doubting the genuineness of their actions. It is impossible to dispute Kendall's influence on several societal concerns, though. Her capacity to draw attention to worthy issues and start meaningful discussions on various subjects has influenced public opinion and promoted constructive change.

Humanitarian Efforts

The role of humanitarian activities is crucial in tackling global issues and promoting constructive transformation. One well-known person who has made a significant entry into the world of philanthropy is Kendall Jenner, who is well-known for her achievements in the entertainment and fashion industries. Even while her achievements in these professions have garnered her widespread recognition, her humanitarian initiatives reveal another aspect of her personality.

Kendall Jenner's entry into the humanitarian field is indicative of a growing trend in which well-known people use their money and notoriety to improve society. Recognizing her power, Jenner has actively backed several organizations, utilizing her position to spread the word and promote worthwhile initiatives. She has made raising awareness of mental health issues one of her main priorities.

Kendall Jenner has committed to dispelling the stigma associated with mental health at a time when mental health problems are becoming more common. She has been transparent about her own experiences, talking about the difficulties she has encountered and stressing the significance of giving mental health priority. By doing this, she has encouraged others to speak up and ask for assistance, fostering a more candid and encouraging conversation around mental health.

Jenner is more than just a talker when it comes to mental health awareness. She has worked with groups that promote mental health awareness and has taken part in campaigns and projects that try to de-stigmatize mental health problems. Her initiatives have struck a chord with her fan base as well as spurred more general discussions about the importance of readily available services and mental health education.

Kendall Jenner has demonstrated a dedication to environmental problems in addition to her work in mental health. Environmental deterioration and climate change are serious worldwide concerns, and celebrities like Jenner have the power to emphasize how urgent it is to solve these problems. She has backed sustainability-related projects, promoting environmentally beneficial behaviors and increasing public understanding of how human activity affects the environment.

Jenner supports environmental problems through her collaborations with companies that value eco-friendly business methods.

She makes a strong statement to her audience and the industry at large about the significance of choosing environmentally friendly products by associating herself with eco-aware businesses. This illustrates how well-known individuals can affect good change by promoting sustainable living through their platform.

In addition to these particular causes, Kendall Jenner has participated in several humanitarian endeavors that tackle larger societal problems. She has demonstrated an adaptable and multidimensional approach to humanitarian action, whether it is through her support of educational initiatives, her advocacy for gender equality, or her participation in disaster relief efforts. Her sincere desire to make a positive impact on the world is evident in her readiness to work with a wide range of causes.

It's critical to remember that there have been some who have criticized Kendall Jenner for her humanitarian work. Stars who participate in charitable endeavors frequently come under fire, with concerns raised over the authenticity of their intentions or the results of their deeds. Nevertheless, it's critical to acknowledge that their participation, independent of public opinion, draws resources and attention to significant causes. It also serves as a reminder that everyone must work together to address complicated global concerns, including prominent leaders and the general people.

Conclusion

The name Kendall Jenner, which has a huge impact outside of reality TV and the fashion industry, is proof of the transformational potential of drive, tenacity, and flexibility. As the fascinating story of Kendall's life comes to an end, it's clear that her path goes beyond fame and wealth to tell a story of transformation and self-discovery.

Kendall's story revolves around an indisputable spirit of perseverance that has taken her from the glitzy reality TV sets to the highly sought-after high fashion catwalk. Being a supermodel and a reality star is no easy achievement, but Kendall's ability to do it with elegance and genuineness has cemented her place in popular culture. With the way that success is defined these days, Kendall's narrative emphasizes how important it is to embrace one's individuality and use it to spur personal development.

In the always-changing and fiercely competitive world of fashion, Kendall Jenner has become more than just a model—she is a force that is changing the norms of what is considered acceptable in the industry. She has been the subject of many famous designers' and photographers' muse due to her statuesque presence and chameleon-like ability to adapt to varied roles. Beyond the flash and glamor, Kendall's success is a testament to her mastery of her art and her dedication to questioning conventional wisdom, pushing the envelope, and, in the end, changing the public's perception of what beauty is.

Kendall's path hasn't been without criticism and difficulties, though. She has been under tremendous public scrutiny due to the weight of her family's past and the ever-present gaze of the media.

However, despite the constant attention, Kendall has proven to be an example of fortitude. She has become even more resilient as a result of her capacity to overcome hardship, including resolving conflict in her family and taking criticism in the design industry. Kendall Jenner is a strong woman in this situation, serving as a reminder to all of us that real resilience comes from a constant dedication to one's path, regardless of the opinions of others.

It is impossible to talk about Kendall's influence without mentioning how she shaped the perception of social media and how it relates to celebrity. Kendall has been leading the way in this evolution of the celebrity paradigm as it has emerged from the internet era. In addition to catapulting her to unprecedented levels of power, her enormous fan base on social media sites like Instagram has completely changed the nature of corporate partnerships and celebrity endorsements. In a time when social media can be a double-edged sword, Kendall has used it to her advantage to connect with her audience, magnify her voice, and support causes that she believes in.

Beyond the social media savvy and fashion runways, Kendall Jenner's charitable activities demonstrate her dedication to changing the world for the better. Kendall has partnered with several nonprofit organizations and used her platform to advocate for social causes, using her power to draw attention to significant worldwide concerns. This activism and sense of duty are reflective of a larger trend among celebrities who understand that their increased stature has the power to bring about positive change.

The voyage of Kendall Jenner, in its essence, is the contemporary odyssey of a young woman negotiating the intricacies of identity, success, and cultural expectations. This is a story that goes beyond the surface levels of celebrity and explores the complexities of authenticity and self-discovery. As we wave farewell to this chapter in Kendall's life story, it is impossible not to be amazed by the depth of her tale—a story that skillfully combines the glittering runway lights with the profound truths discovered in the furnace of public scrutiny.

The glossy pages of fashion magazines and the pixels on a smartphone screen are just little portions of her legacy. It is proof of the human spirit's tenacity, the strength of reinvention, and the capacity to reinvent oneself in the middle of a world that is ever-changing. Her story inspires us to consider our pathways, embrace our individuality, face obstacles head-on, and pursue authenticity in a society that frequently rewards conformity. When we put the finishing touches on Kendall Jenner's biography thus far, we find that it is more than just the story of a supermodel; rather, it is a story of empowerment, growth, and the unwavering spirit of a woman who has made a lasting impression on modern culture.